Come for a down the Amazon River in Peru and discover a world of pink dolphins, man-eating fish and much more...

Copyright © 2022 by Arranging Clouds

All rights reserved. No part of this book may be reproduced or used in any manner without written permission of the copyright owner except for the use of quotations in a book review. For more information, address: arrangingclouds@gmail.com

FIRST EDITION

My Amazon Adventure

By Katherine Buckley

Last year, my mum and I embarked on a trip of a lifetime and travelled to the Amazon Rainforest, in Peru.

To get there, we took two flights. It was very exciting and tiring.

On the aeroplane, I sat in the window seat and I took this photograph.

The Andean Mountains or The Andes are the longest mountain range in the world. The highest mountain in South America is found in Argentina. In Peru, the highest mountain is called Huascarán. It reaches 6,768 metres high.

On the first day, we took a boat along the Amazon River to our lodge.

The Amazon river is found in South America. It originates in Peru and travels through Ecuador, Columbia, Venezuela, Bolivia and Brazil before reaching the Atlantic Ocean.

We boarded a small wooden river boat called a 'canoa'. The journey took a couple of hours.

The next morning, we got up early to go fishing for piranhas and to search for pink river dolphins.

There are many species of piranhas in the Amazon river. The most common is the red-bellied piranha which has the strongest jaw and sharpest teeth of all. Although piranhas can attack people, it is more likely that humans hunt piranhas to eat.

I caught a piranha and touched its pointy, sharp teeth. Then I threw it back into the river.

On the way back to our lodge, a family of pink dolphins surrounded our boat.

Mum said it was thrilling!

Amazon river dolphins are the largest freshwater dolphin. They can grow up to 9ft (2.7 metres) long. Their brains are bigger than human brains. Unfortunately, they are an endangered species.. They are often hunted for fishing bait and are suffering due to environmental pollution.

There are many myths surrounding the pink river dolphins. Some people say they can transform into men. These mythical creatures are called 'boto' by the local people.

The next day, mum and I visited a monkey sanctuary.

I bought a postcard of a sloth to send to my grandma.

Sloths live in the rainforests of Central and South America. Sometimes they lose their homes due to deforestation.

A monkey climbed up onto my shoulder and I held an anaconda.

At the sanctuary, there was a strange-looking river turtle, a sloth, snakes and some parrots and toucans, too.

The water boa or green anaconda is one of the largest snakes in the world. They are not poisonous but kill their prey by suffocating it or by dragging it underwater.

The anaconda has no natural predator except for man. They are killed for their skin or because people think they are dangerous.

On the third day of our trip, we visited some Amazonian tribal villages.

We visited the Bora Tribe and The Yagua Tribe. They live in villages up and down the Amazon River.

The tribes live in communities of several families. It is often the men who wear skirts made out of palm-tree fibre.

I played football with some of the native children from the village and later I bought a blowpipe as a souvenir.

There were many souvenirs to buy from the local people. They use seeds to make into bags, necklaces and bracelets. They crochet hammocks using palm-tree fibre. I liked this blowpipe or 'pucuna' best. The local tribesmen use this weapon to hunt monkeys, porcupines, sloths and birds.

On our final morning in the Amazon Rainforest, we visited a salt lick.

As the sun rose, lots of brightly coloured birds came to lick the salt. I saw parakeets, macaws and parrots.

It was incredible!

A salt lick or mineral lick is a deposit of mineral salts used by animals to supplement their diet. Many animals use salt licks to get essential nutrients like calcium, magnesium, sodium, and zinc.

When we got back home, I chose the best photographs from my trip to pin on my bedroom wall.

I will remember that amazing trip all my life!

These are two of my favourite photos from my trip. I chose the photograph of the Amazon River because it looks like an anaconda and the photo of the pink river dolphin because they are extremely rare and in danger of extinction.

Printed in Great Britain
by Amazon